REFLECTION THROUGH THE
MIRROR

---

by

Denise M. Thomas

Gotham Books

30 N Gould St.
Ste. 20820, Sheridan, WY 82801
https://gothambooksinc.com/

Phone: 1 (307) 464-7800

© 2024 *Denise M. Thomas*. All rights reserved.

No part of this book may be reproduced, stored in a retrieval system, or transmitted by any means without the written permission of the author.

All Scriptures from the King James Version. Public Domain.

Any people depicted in stock imagery provided by Thinkstock are models, and such images are being used for illustrative purposes only. Certain stock imagery © Thinkstock.

Published by Gotham Books (April 10, 2024)

ISBN: 979-8-88775-902-9 (H)
ISBN: 979-8-88775-743-8 (P)
ISBN: 979-8-88775-744-5 (E)

Because of the dynamic nature of the Internet, any web addresses or links contained in this book may have changed since publication and may no longer be valid.

The views expressed in this work are solely those of the author and do not necessarily reflect the views of the publisher, and the publisher hereby disclaims any responsibility for them.

CONTENTS

Reflection 1
Love Yourself 3
Grow in Faith 5
Dump the Weights 7
Goals and Challenges 9
Life is Possible with Jesus 11
Believe It 13
Forgive Others 15
Love Unlimited 17
Faith is Real 19
Soar 21
Sovereignty 23
Peace in the Valley 25
Renewal 27
Lord, Lord! 32

This book is dedicated to my beloved mother Beatrice.
Thanks to my husband, Terry, for all his support and love.

Reflection

What would Jesus do? What a question? This is a very small sentence with a huge meaning. I look for a higher meaning daily. Why am I here? What is my purpose? Am I living my life to the fullest? Are we just a specimen in a huge bowl?

Where there is love, there is life. Where there is life, there is hope. Where there is hope, there is faith. Where there is faith, miracles happen. Where there is peace, there is God. And when you have God, you have everything.

Amen

Love Yourself

How would I know I never did this before? Life feels like a merry go round, get up, get ready, here comes the next turn, round and round we go. When I was eight years old I discovered Jesus. I was not inside a church or surrounded by people. It was one of the scarcest days of my life. I was afraid for my mother. You see my stepfather was an alcoholic a man that worked 5 days a week, and came home four days out of seven. Sorry maybe I should say four in a half days he always made it back on Sunday evening with not a cent in his pocket. This story is not about an abusive alcoholic or a drunkard broken man, it is about how it shaped my life.

Grow in Faith

I grew up in a small town in Tennessee where in the summer it was hot enough to fry eggs on the sidewalk if you had one. Life was good so I thought, how was I to know everyone did not live like me. I was given responsibilities which I took pride in, why shouldn't I; my parents trusted me to take care of my siblings. Little did I know that this would be a life or death sentence? No matter how old they are it's your duty to keep an eye on them. You do know everybody grows up at a different time, and it never happens when you want it. My life was full of fun memories, I had five brothers that were my knight in shining armor. Life was not a bed of roses, which is not a place I would want to be anyway. Roses have thorns.

Dump the Weights

Sometimes life just isn't fair; we learned that at an early age. Our parents tell us to go to church! go to church! Where you find people all dressed up and sitting pretty, looking like they do not have a care in the world. It's wonderful to know that all you have to do is go to church.

Goals and Challenges

As I said before I was an eight-year-old when I found the Lord and it was not at church. I went to church. It was one of the places that I was allowed to go. You see my mother ruled our house, yes there was a father present but she was our solid foundation. She did not work out of the home, and the reason could be that she has so many little ones. I just don't happen to believe it, because when she made her mind up, to go to work after leaving my step father she went. You will never find a prouder mother than mine. You see her sibling and she was brought up that way, her grandparents raise them to have respect for themselves, never to think anyone was better than they were. It did not matter what you did for living, you did it to the best of your ability. Your home is your sanctuary, no matter if it was a one room stack it was to be clean and cared for, the yard cleaned with grass or no grass, get a broom!

Life is Possible with Jesus

An Excuse was just that excuse, the words my mother used," they are like ass holes everyone has one". She had a lot of saying and I am sure they were from her grandparents, because her parents died when she was nine. Life is like that sometime, good time and bad. It's how you react that changes your life, negative reactions give negative responses, positive leads to great responses because they make you stronger not bitter. "I love the Lord he heard my cry". Praise him in the good times and the bad. How great it is when we grab the hands of the Father that loves us. It's great when you learn the only hand that will keep you is His.

Believe It

Forgive and forget how hard it is when you have been violated. The hurt and heartache is so powerful, that you feel like it's an out of body experience. There are times that your mind play tricks on you. You begin to understand that it is the Lord that is shielding you from the pain. This is why you can continue at that time, unfortunately you will have to return to the painful reality, and remember and then forgive. Don't misunderstand me forgiving is not forgetting, which takes a longer time and much later.

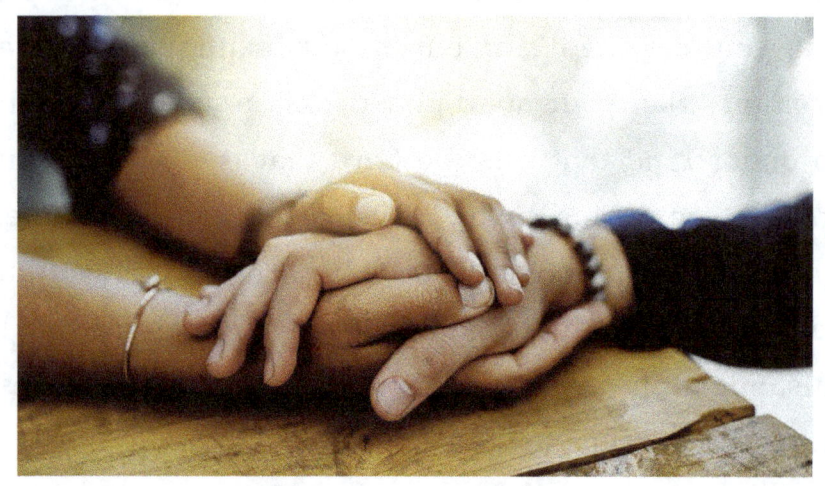

Forgive Others

I wish that pain and suffering was not a part of this world. Some experiences of pain are weapons that increase our faith, for we know that we must suffer in order to make it a greater blessing. Do not confuse unjustified killing of each other, hate of your neighbor and knowing that you are not living a life that is pleasing to God. What God is teaching us, we are to learn from our suffering like Paul; suffer for the glory of the Lord and learn to lean and depend on him? Life is not a bed of roses, which is just a saying; it does not work like that.

Love Unlimited

Learn to pray and to dream each day. Tell your children to dream and have hope, no matter what the situation. Hope comes from above and dreams come from within.

No matter the road blocks, always hold on to your dreams. Make a list each time you achieve something and check it off and add something else. I know this sounds strange, but it works I am a witness, please don't start your list with things you can't achieve at the level where you are at that time. Small steps or still steps, watch the baby smile when you clap. I was not born with money and silver slippers, living was hard. My parent's life was hard; clothing, feeding, shelter and work were not a given. They had to have faith to take one day at a time, and put one foot in front of the other. Keep pushing, hold your head up, and do the best you can until things get better. No! change does not happen when we want it, but keep doing and living like it will. Remember each person must support the other, have we forgotten how to do that, get your family back together and be open and for real. Keep God first and remember how having families used to mean something. I was a dreamer and these are the things I did, thanks to my mom.

Faith is Real

I don't know, have you looked in the mirror lately? Do you like what you see? Hopefully you do. We can't change the world but we can change ourselves. Stop shouting at your children, they will shout, stop hating yourself for things you have no control; your children will hate and have no control. Stop wanting material things more than God, your children will do whatever it takes to get them. The things that are going on in the world today are not new, talking with an elderly person is not something they haven't seen. They will tell you that children are not respectful as they used to be. The funny thing is they just didn't use the words around their elders, not that they did not do it.

My mom used to say children are to be seen and not heard, what she was telling us was that children do not need to be involved in adult conversation or business.

Soar

Yes, I do believe there are a lot of challenges facing children today. But we have to remember that children see and hear a lot more now than in the fifties. The things that are going on with children are distressing, that humans created in God's image are so evil? When I look at this I always think about Eve in the garden where sin began. In my mind I see Eve looking at Satan, and then I began to wonder what attract her to him. Before the eating of the fruit how often did she talk with him, was Adam aware of this? It's funny how we as people do not listen persistently, I tell my husband that I believe most people are afraid of being alone.

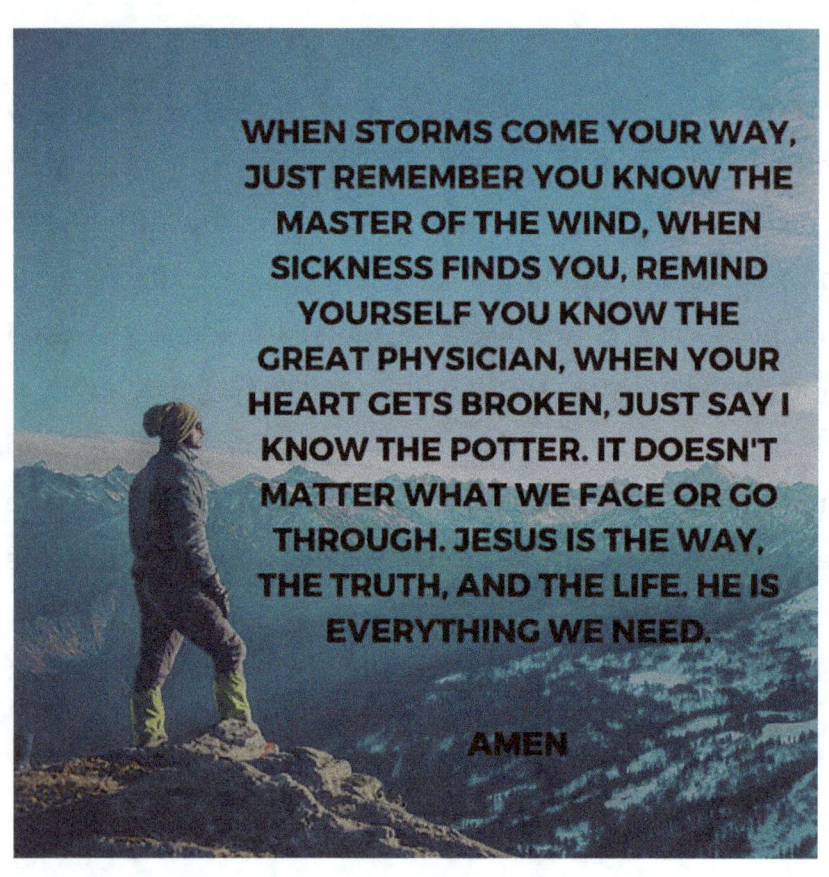

Sovereignty

We have so many things in the world to distract us like TV, movies, radio, and cell phone. We will find someone or something to keep us away from the silence. Was that Eve's problem? Why was she talking with Satan? That is so fascinating to me. Be assured the answer is already given this was in the Planning. Humans are weak creatures that continue to fall, until God intervenes and rescues us. It is not easy trying to live a life that is worthy of God, but thank God he is right there with us. And all Eve had to do was call out to him, the same as we must do. Trouble on every hand, yes we will have trials and tribulations that are to make us more dependent on God. Eve just confirmed that having everything still is not enough for us. Do we know how to be happy with what we have? Did Eve curiosity get the best of her? Well you know what they say "curiosity killed the cat" And if we don't get our acts together it will kill us too, just in a bigger frying pan.

Peace in the Valley

What is the secret? How do we become dependent? Some people would call that lazy, complacent, looking for a hand out. Turning over your life to God is totally different than working on a job, this in itself is a JOB letting go and letting God, is hard work for us humans. Just take a deep breath does that feel good? How do you think it would feel to have that renewed feeling every day? Maybe like "Peace in the valley of the shadow of death". Just wondering, let your imaginations fly.

Renewal

My imagination was my greatest gift while I was growing up, and reading was how it became possible. I dreamed of a different life and it took effort to make it happen. My desire was just not to be afraid, God made that possible at the age of eight. As I grew older it was something that I held onto with both hands, sometimes not sure what or who was helping me. You see at eight I knew of God, but not until I developed a relationship did I understand that my prayer life was stronger than just one night it was a life line.

"Be strong and of good courage, and do it: fear not, nor be dismayed."

1 Chronicles 28:20

He was showing and giving me the desires of my heart, with tears in my eyes I reflected upon those things. How precious is the love of God for his children, who believe he loves us in all of our trials and tribulation? Through life we have to hold onto that belief with firm determination without doubt. He didn't say it was going to be easy just keep your eyes on the prize of his promise of eternal life. This is my journey and it has been over fifty years. Can you read this without negativity? Well, just look in your mirror and start your journey, restart, rebuild, forgive, forget, love, love again. Only you can make you happy.

Don't let pass mistakes and hurts stop you from dreaming and achieving. Believe it or not sometime you have to put yourself in a position to try. How else will you know if you don't try? You may fail so what, it's better than "I always planned on trying".

My mother would tell me that I was never satisfied, because I was always changing jobs, I never disagree with her, because I knew when I found the right one it would be great. I knew that what I learned from one job would help with the next. Life is like that, use everything you learned or experienced, don't let it go to waste. Mother used to say don't cry over thing you can't control, do something about it. So I would prepare myself for the next journey in my life, like I said set limits, go to school, take an online class, whatever it takes.

    Everything is not for everybody; you have to look deep at your reflection in the mirror, determine what is for you. Be honest with yourself, and don't worry this is for you.

Lord, Lord!

Lord, Lord! Can you be honest with yourself? We can make excuses for ourselves, and others help us. Look at your reflection in the mirror if you look long enough tears may fall from your eyes. The heart will tell you the truth no matter what others may say. It can be hard when self is revealed, praise God we have a savior that sees us and still loves us and leads us through the rough patches. Oh, no it is not a wish bowl fantasy, it's life that requires work, getting yourself together with God's help, going to a quiet corner, your bedroom, or in the car. "Fear thou not, for I am with thee be not dismayed; for I am thy God: I will strengthen thee; yea, I will help thee with the right hand of my righteousness" (Isaiah 41:10) Yes, we all get caught up, just don't give up, keep looking for that light. Don't ever think God has given up on you, He is just a prayer away. Pray about your situation, pray for Godly counsel, pray for a way out, pray for your children, grandchildren, spouse, family and friend also your enemy, don't forget to add your name. That was my problem, I would pray for everyone but myself. I thought it was selfish to pray for myself until I learned better. Did you know that everybody doesn't pray for you, even when you ask. Don't worry God has us covered from the top of our head to the bottom of our feet.

This knowledge brings me so much happiness, I love knowing God is there for you and me. I want everybody to know He is real and personal. Please don't give up, He really does love us. Do you know anybody that when you ask sincerely, will give you something without expecting a monetary payment? You do have to decide to receive it and you must say Thank You. Mother always said to say thank you for good gifts. No one can tell you what God has instore for us, we must ask him. Let me tell you something God knows because he created us (Genesis 2:7,18,21-23). He knows we will make mistakes, take the wrong road but all we must do is look to him for help, but it's our decision humans can be stubborn and selfish. God is a patience God that will wait until you are tired of doing it your way. How is life going for you??

Notes:

www.ingramcontent.com/pod-product-compliance
Lightning Source LLC
LaVergne TN
LVHW020420070526
838199LV00055B/3675